TEAM
HOYT

"Yes You Can"

Rick's Story - The Story of Rick Hoyt

Copyright © 2009 by Dick Hoyt

Printed in the United States.

ISBN-13: 978-1-934878-87-3
ISBN-10: 1-934878-87-1

Mascot Books
560 Herndon Parkway #120, Herndon, VA 20170

www.mascotbooks.com

Have a book idea? Contact us at:
Mascot Books
P.O. Box 220157
Chantilly, VA 20153-0157
info@mascotbooks.com

I dedicate this book to my Mom, Dad, my brothers, Rob and Russ, and to all my teachers and professors who encouraged me to never give up and always keep trying. Thanks to all the doctors and therapists that have helped me. And finally, to all the personal care assistants I have had over the years that have helped me live an independent life - thank you!

- Rick Hoyt

"To: Riley

"Enjoy The Book"

Rich 4/14/12

I dedicate this book to my colleague and friend, Denise Porcello. She first developed the idea for this book, suggested it to the Hoyt's, and recommended me as the author. Thanks for helping make a dream come true!

~Sherrie Ninteau

Rick's Story

The Story of Rick Hoyt

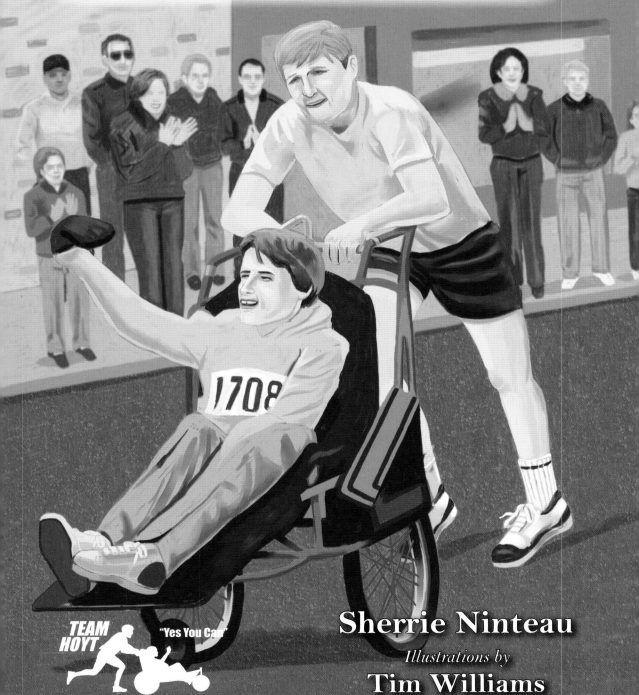

Sherrie Ninteau

Illustrations by
Tim Williams

TEAM
HOYT
"Yes You Can"

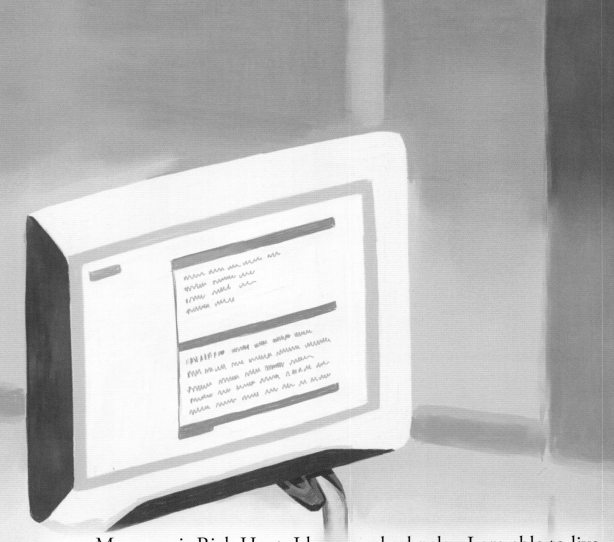

My name is Rick Hoyt. I have cerebral palsy. I am able to live in my own apartment. I have traveled across the United States and to many places around the world. I would like to tell you about how I have lived with this challenge I was born with and how I have followed my dreams.

The first thing you may notice about me is that I sit in a wheelchair. This is because I am not able to control my arms or my legs. It means that I need someone to help me get around. With the support of my family and my personal care assistants, I am able to lead a very active life.

I do not speak like you, but I understand everything you say to me. I use a special computer that helps me "talk" to you. It has a stick that I push with my head to type the words I want to say. The computer then says my words out loud.

I may look and sound different from you, but inside we are just the same. I think and feel things just like you. At times, I feel sadness. Other times, I feel joy. I feel love, compassion, and pain. I love to hear a good joke and I'm known to be a jokester. People know what I am feeling by looking into my eyes. My parents always said my eyes told those things my voice was unable to say.

My parents wanted me to be treated like any other child while I was growing up. Mom realized I was smart and began teaching me the alphabet when I was very young. She did this by cutting letters from sandpaper and tracing my fingers over each one. We did this every day and soon I knew my letters. She also put signs on things around my house. She labeled things like "window" and "door," and I began to associate the words with objects.

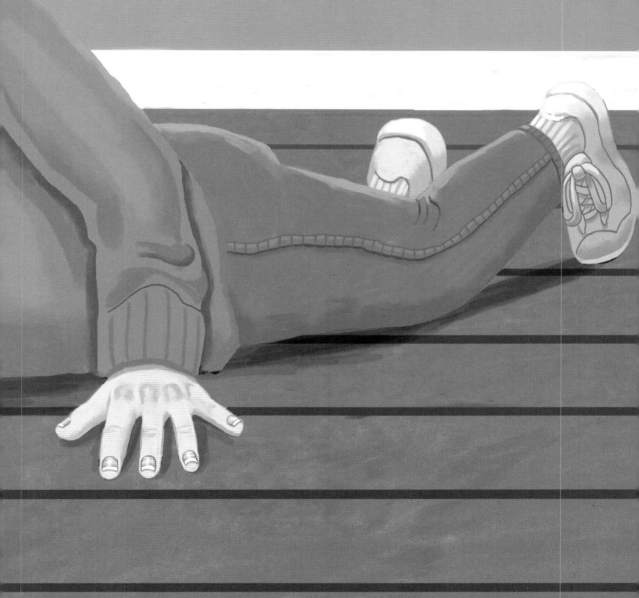

It takes me a long time but I can now type what I want to say. I remember my family's reaction when I typed my first message. I told you I love a good joke. They were all watching me type, letter by letter, using my head movements. Each one of them was betting on what my first words would be.

Mom's guess was, "Hi, Mom!"

Dad guessed, "Hi, Dad!"

My brothers, Rob and Russell, had other guesses. I fooled them as I slowly typed out "G-O-B-R." No one could figure it out. Can you? It says, "Go Bruins!" I'm a big fan of the Boston Bruins, a professional hockey team. I nearly jumped out of my seat laughing! They never would have guessed.

My brother, Russell, helped me develop another method to talk. We called it the "Russell Method." He broke the alphabet into five blocks, each beginning with a vowel. The first block contained the letters A through D; the second block contained the letters E through H. When I needed to say something, I let them know which letter it started with, quickly going through the blocks until we came to the right section. This cut down on the time it took to spell out my message.

Growing up, I did many things with my family. I went camping, hiking, cross-country skiing, and swimming. I was included in every family activity. When we would go swimming, my brothers would throw me into the pool then jump in and hold me up so I could breathe. You should have seen people's faces when this happened! I trusted my brothers though and it taught me not to fear the water.

As a young boy, I attended public schools. I wanted to be treated the same as all the other kids. My sixth grade physical education teacher really made this happen. He insisted that I attend his gym class. Before this, I had to go to the library while my friends went to gym. I really love sports and being able to participate in them with my friends was awesome! My teacher made up some new games just for me! I was able to play while my classmates pushed me in my wheelchair. It felt so good to be part of the group.

I was at a basketball game with my gym teacher when I saw something that changed my life forever. It was a poster that read:

Run for Doogie
Use Your Legs to Help His!
Show Your Favorite Midfielder Your Love
Fundraiser 5-Mile Road Race on Saturday

Doogie was a member of the lacrosse team who became paralyzed while playing the game. I knew what he felt like and wanted to help. I couldn't wait to get home to ask Dad to run the race with me! Dad said, "Okay!" but he wasn't a runner. We sure surprised everyone when we crossed the finish line. It was a great feeling! Dad was pushing me in my wheelchair and my arms were flying in the air as a sign of our victory! Dad said that I had the biggest smile on my face that anyone had ever seen. I told him, "When I'm running, I feel like I'm not even disabled!"

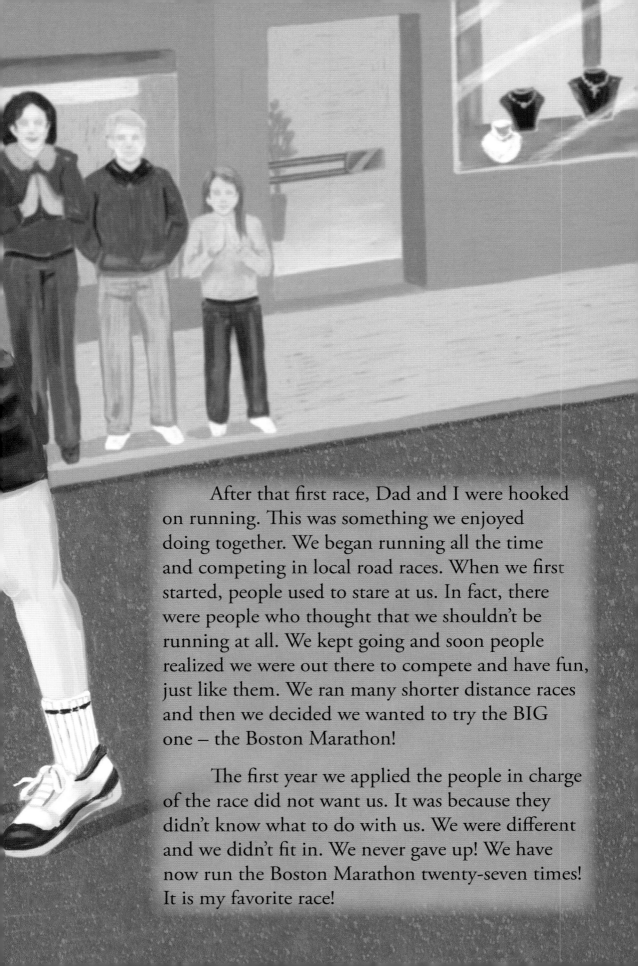

After that first race, Dad and I were hooked on running. This was something we enjoyed doing together. We began running all the time and competing in local road races. When we first started, people used to stare at us. In fact, there were people who thought that we shouldn't be running at all. We kept going and soon people realized we were out there to compete and have fun, just like them. We ran many shorter distance races and then we decided we wanted to try the BIG one – the Boston Marathon!

The first year we applied the people in charge of the race did not want us. It was because they didn't know what to do with us. We were different and we didn't fit in. We never gave up! We have now run the Boston Marathon twenty-seven times! It is my favorite race!

Dad and I also compete in triathlons. This type of race combines swimming, biking, and running. Dad pulls, pumps, and pushes me along using special equipment which allows me to be with him. He swims with me lying in a raft attached to him by straps, pumps our bicycle that has a front seat attachment, and pushes me in a special running chair. Every step of the way has been an adventure! Dad and I have competed in triathlons all over the world. We have competed in Canada, Japan, El Salvador, and Germany, but the most difficult one for us was in Hawaii.

The Ironman Hawaii Championship is the most challenging triathlon in the world. It requires competitors to swim 2.4 miles in the ocean, ride a bike 112 miles, and run a full 26.2 mile marathon – all in the same day! We first swam in the Pacific Ocean, and then biked up mountains that were formed over many years by volcanoes. Our swim went well, but our bike had a problem – our brakes gave out. This happened right on the top of the highest mountain! We waited in the blazing heat until a crew came to help us. Both Dad and I were very tired, hot, and thirsty. When my dad asked me if I wanted to go on, I nodded my head, "Yes," and off we went! It was already dark before we started the marathon run. The hills were tough, but in the end, Dad was running and passing other participants. We finished the race with our arms raised over our heads. Team Hoyt had done it again! We successfully completed the Ironman Hawaii Triathlon!

In 1992, we started an organization to benefit disabled people called the "Hoyt Foundation." Our goal was to make every building in America accessible to people with disabilities. In order to raise money and awareness, Dad and I took on a courageous challenge. We decided to bike across the United States from Santa Monica, California to Boston, Massachusetts!

We biked and ran about 90 miles each day, and reached Boston Harbor in 45 days! Before we left California, we filled a champagne bottle with water from the Pacific Ocean. When we reached Boston, we poured that bottle of water into the Atlantic Ocean. It was a symbol that connected people with disabilities from coast to coast.

Shortly after completing our "Trek Across America," I graduated from college. It took me nine long years, but I stuck with it! In 1993 – at the age of 31 – I graduated from Boston University with a degree in Special Education. I am one of the few people with my disability to have graduated from a university! I am very proud of this.

I have had so many incredible experiences in my life. I've done things that most people only dream about. I try my hardest at everything I do. No matter how hard things become, I never give up! I know I can do anything I put my mind to! I hope my story has helped you to understand that people with physical challenges are thinking, feeling, and caring people, just like you! It's up to all of us to work together so each and every person can become the best that they can be!

About the author

Sherrie teaches fourth grade at the Brookside Elementary School in Dracut, Massachusetts. She is a runner and a triathlete. Her first time meeting Rick was at a running club meeting. She was so inspired by Rick's story that she invited him to come to speak to the students at her school. Parents, staff, and students were so moved by Rick and his father, Dick, that it was suggested a children's book be written to tell their story. This began a three year relationship with the Hoyt's that has helped her fulfill a dream of becoming an author. She hopes that "Rick's Story" will leave you feeling that you can achieve your dreams, too.

About the illustrator

Tim Williams has been an award winning freelance illustrator for over twenty-five years. From whimsical humorous illustration to dead-on realism, Tim offers a wide variety of styles from which to choose.

His work has been seen on magazine covers, in magazines, on posters, in advertising campaigns and on book covers. Tim has also illustrated fifteen children's books. Tim has also been the illustrator for three different humor books.

Tim lives in Cumming, Georgia with his wife Donna. They have a married daughter Whitney, who is an art director in Atlanta.